YONDE KAITE

よんでかいて

JAPANESE WORKBOOK

PRIMARY LEVEL 2

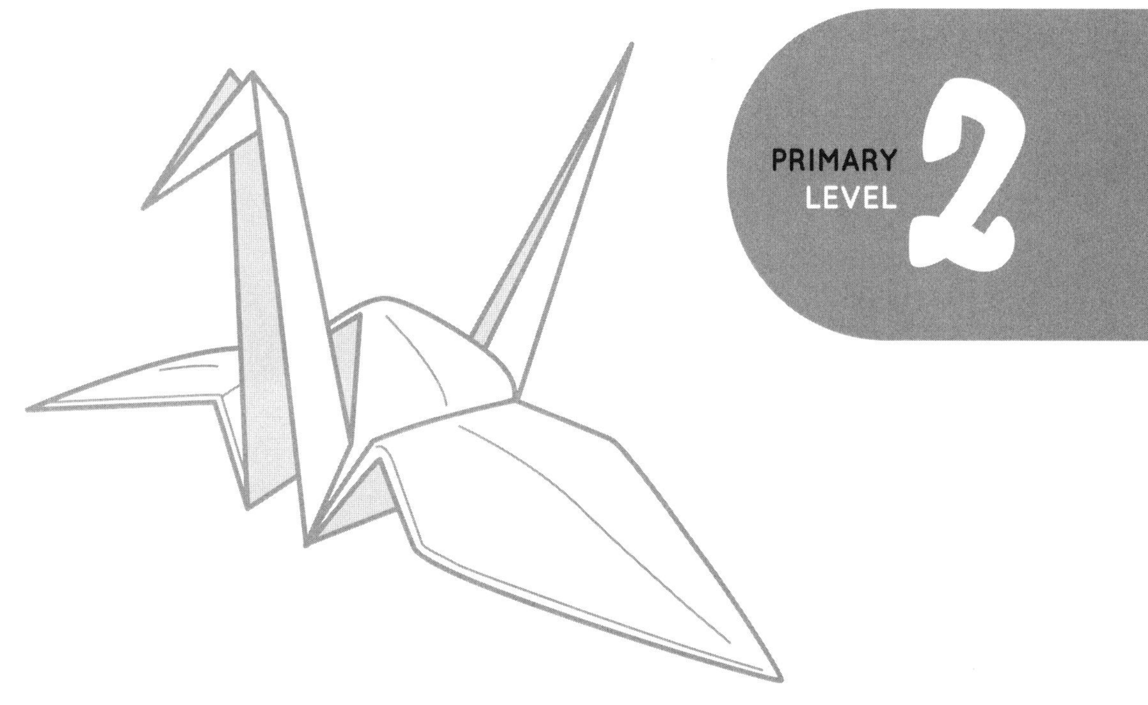

WRITTEN BY

ANNE RAJAKUMAR

WITH ORIGINAL ILLUSTRATIONS BY

JENNIFER CHENG

First published in 1999, reprinted in 2001, 2003, 2007, 2008, 2009, 2010, 2011, 2012, 2016, 2017 This redesigned edition first published in 2017, reprinted in 2019, 2020, 2022, 2023.

Insight Publications Pty Ltd
3/350 Charman Road
Cheltenham Victoria 3192
Australia

Tel: +61 3 8571 4950
Fax: +61 3 8571 0257
Email: books@insightpublications.com.au

www.insightpublications.com.au

ISBN: 9781875882205

Illustrations by Jennifer Cheng; other images courtesy of Shutterstock
Cover and internal design by Gisela Beer
Proofing by Sage Napthine-Morrison and Fabrice Wilmann

Printed by Markono Print Media Pte Ltd

Author acknowledgements
Special thanks to my family, Kumar, Timothy and Jessica, for their constant support and assistance and to Barbara and Chris for their untiring advice and unwavering encouragement and help.

Table of Contents

LANGUAGE AND EXTENSION LESSONS

WRITING LESSONS

日本語

わたし は	I (used by girls)
ぼく は	I (used by boys)

です	am
さい	years old

一	1	三	3	五	5	七	7	九	9
二	2	四	4	六	6	八	8	十	10

Trace over the Japanese words and write your name in the appropriate box.

(girls) わたし は  です。

(boys) ぼく は 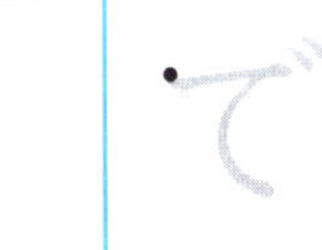 です。

Draw a picture of something you like, then trace over the Japanese words underneath and write your age in the appropriate box.

(girls) わたし は  さいです。

(boys) ぼく は  さいです。

わたし は	I (used by girls)
ぼく は	I (used by boys)

です	am
さい	years old

一	1	三	3	五	5	七	7	九	9
二	2	四	4	六	6	八	8	十	10

Trace over the Japanese words, then write each sentence in English. Kai's speech box is done for you.

ぼく は Kai です。
I am Kai.
ぼく は 七 さい です。
I am 7 years old.

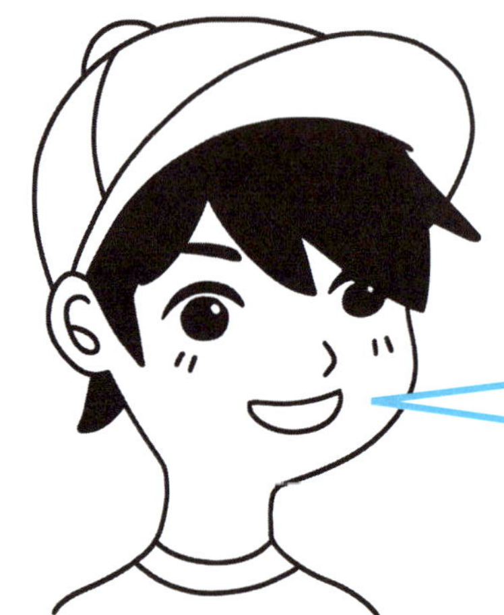

ぼく は Blake です。

____

ぼく は 八 さい です。

____

わたし は Mia です。

____

わたし は 六 さい です。

____

Trace over the word for Japan, then colour in your map.

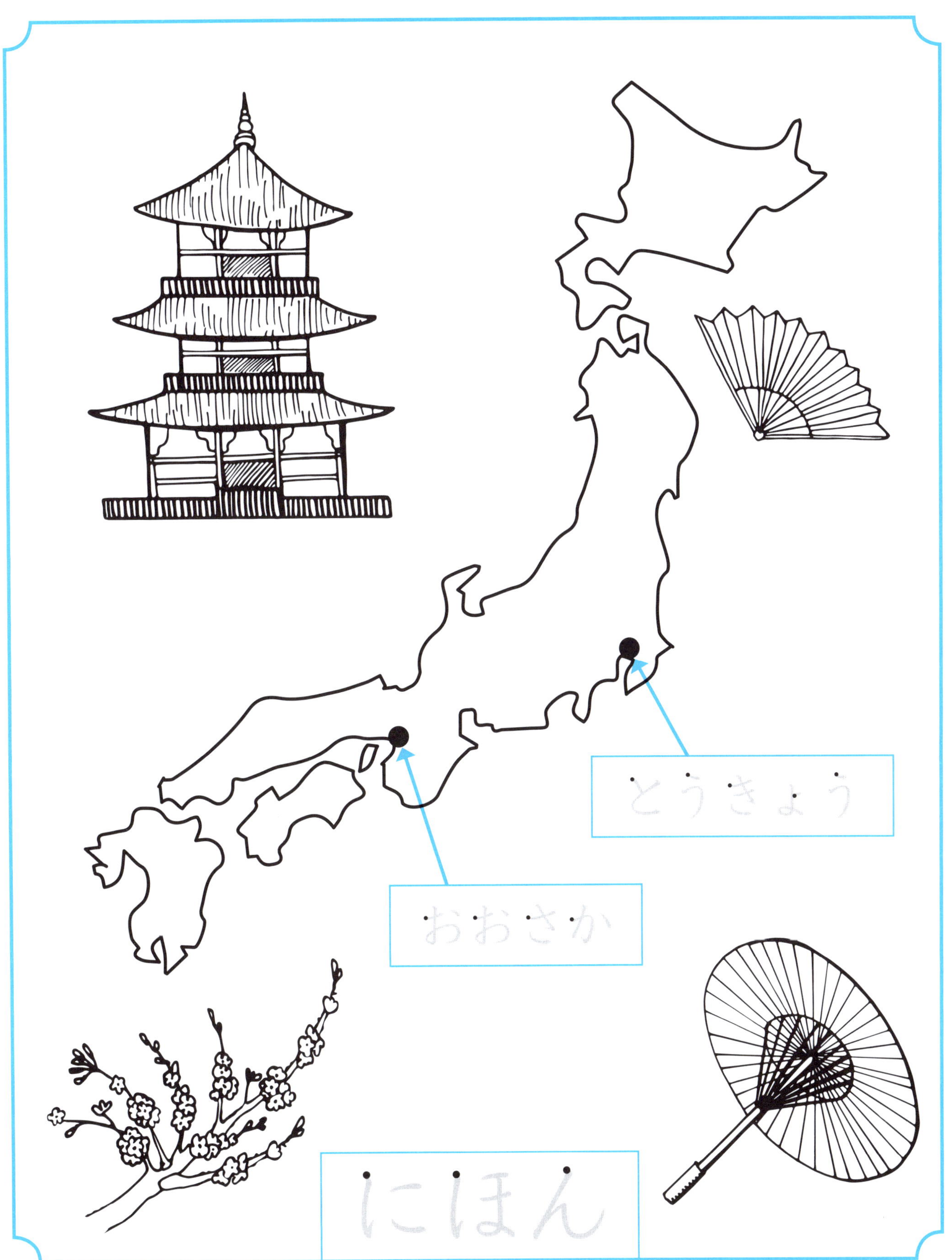

一	1
二	2
三	3
四	4
五	5

六	6
七	7
八	8
九	9
十	10

十	一	11
十	二	12
十	三	13
十	四	14
十	五	15

十	六	16
十	七	17
十	八	18
十	九	19
二	十	20

See how many sums you can do. Trace over the Japanese numbers, then write your answers in Japanese.

一 + 二 =

三 + 一 =

二 + 一 =

三 + 二 =

六 + 三 =

四 + 二 =

八 + 六 =

十 + 五 =

八 + 三 =

五 + 五 =

七 + 八 =

九 + 四 =

九 + 八 =

六 + 七 =

おはよう ございます	good morning
こんにちは	hello (good day)
こんばんは	good evening
おやすみ なさい	goodnight
さようなら	goodbye

Trace over the greeting words, then colour the greeting pictures.

おはよう ございます

こんにちは

こんばんは

おやすみ なさい

さようなら

おはよう ございます	good morning
こんにち は	hello (good day)
こんばん は	good evening
おやすみ なさい	goodnight
さようなら	goodbye

Trace over the Japanese words, then write what was said in English underneath.

こんにちは

こんにちは

What did they say? ______________________________

おはよう
ございます

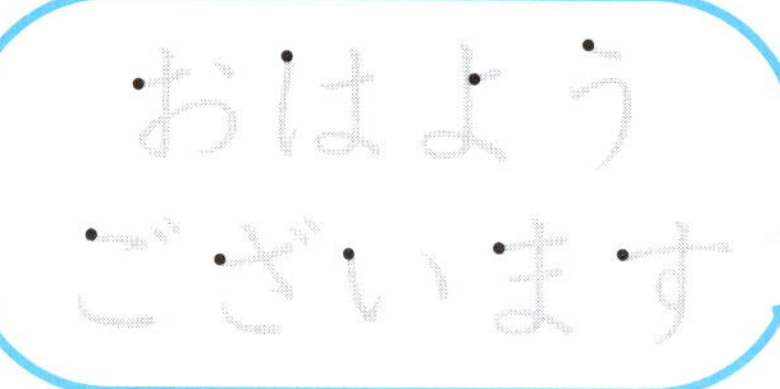

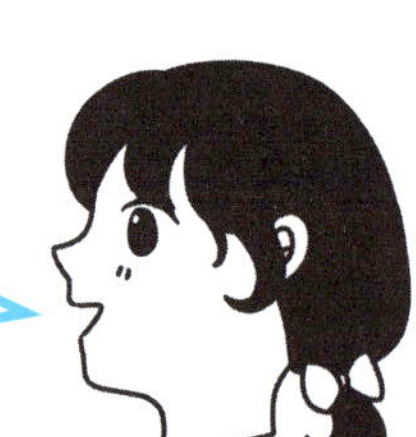

What did they say? ______________________________

こんばんは

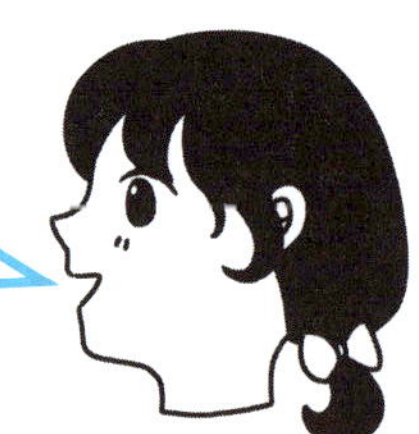

What did they say? ______________________________

おやすみ
なさい

What did they say? ______________________________

おとうさん	father
おかあさん	mother
おにいさん	older brother
おねえさん	older sister

おとうと	younger brother
いもうと	younger sister
あかちゃん	baby

Trace over the family words, then colour in the family pictures.

おとうさん

おにいさん

おねえさん

おかあさん

いもうと

あかちゃん

おとうと

おとうさん	father
おかあさん	mother
おにいさん	older brother
おねえさん	older sister

おとうと	younger brother
いもうと	younger sister
あかちゃん	baby

Trace over the correct family word under each picture.

おとうさん
おかあさん

いもうと
おとうと

あかちゃん
おかあさん

おにいさん
おかあさん

あかちゃん
おにいさん

おねえさん
おとうさん

いもうと
おとうと

げつようび	Monday
かようび	Tuesday
すいようび	Wednesday
もくようび	Thursday

きんようび	Friday
どようび	Saturday
にちようび	Sunday

Colour in the day of the week words. Shade 

a special colour.

THE DAY OF THE WEEK ROCK RAP

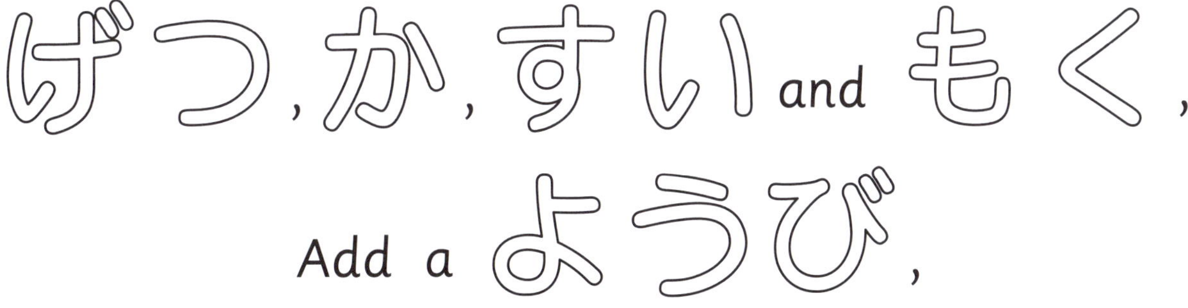

That's the day of the week rock.

Then comes きん, ど and にち

Makes my hands and feet feel itchy!

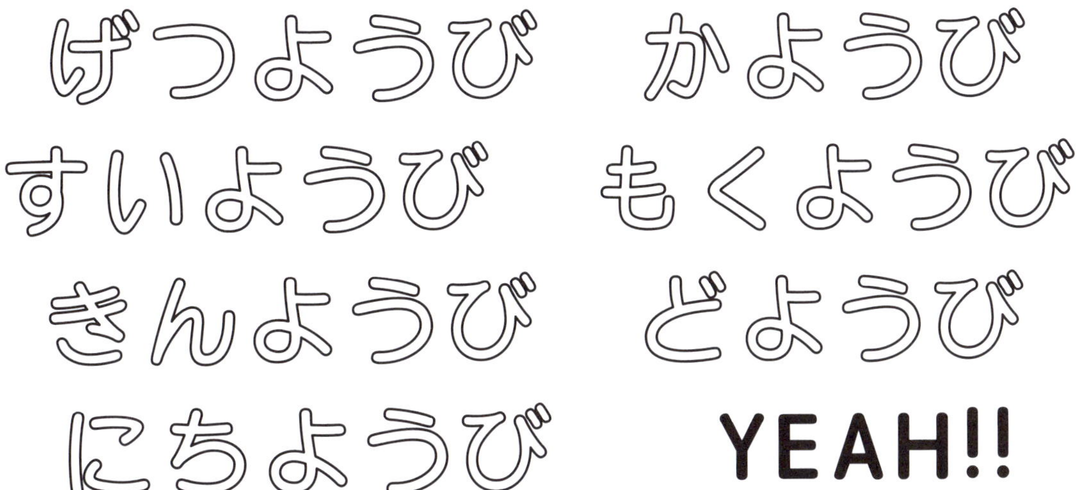

げつようび	Monday
かようび	Tuesday
すいようび	Wednesday
もくようび	Thursday

きんようび	Friday
どようび	Saturday
にちようび	Sunday

Trace over the hiragana words, then join the balloons to their owners.

げつようび

かようび

もくようび

すいようび

どようび

にちようび

きんようび

Sunday

Saturday

Monday

Wednesday

Thursday

Friday

Tuesday

ほん	book	いす	chair
えんぴつ	pencil	つくえ	desk
かみ	paper	せんせい	teacher
けしゴム	eraser	はさみ	scissors
ものさし	ruler	こども	child

Trace over the classroom words.

ほん	book
えんぴつ	pencil
かみ	paper
けしゴム	eraser
ものさし	ruler

いす	chair
つくえ	desk
せんせい	teacher
はさみ	scissors
こども	child

Draw a picture of each object, then trace over the label.

かみ	
けしゴム	
ものさし	
はさみ	
せんせい	

つくえ	
ほん	
いす	
えんぴつ	
こども	

☺☺☺ を ください。	Please give me ☺☺☺.
どうぞ。	Here you are.
ありがとう。	Thank you.

Taka asks Hana for a book. Hana gives Taka the book. Taka thanks Hana.

Trace over the Japanese words.

ほんをください。

どうぞ。

ありがとう。

What is the Japanese word for book?

What is the Japanese word for thank you?

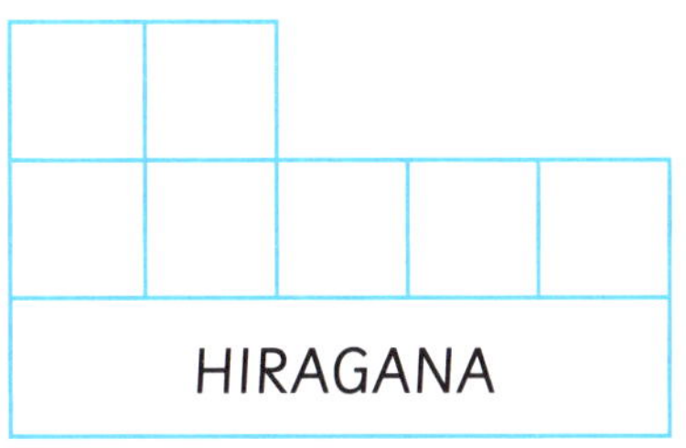

ほん	book
えんぴつ	pencil
かみ	paper
けしゴム	eraser
ものさし	ruler

いす	chair
つくえ	desk
せんせい	teacher
はさみ	scissors
こども	child

Trace over the hiragana, then join the matching English and Japanese words.

ほん	pencil
ものさし	eraser
かみ	child
こども	teacher
せんせい	book
つくえ	scissors
いす	chair
えんぴつ	paper
けしゴム	ruler
はさみ	desk

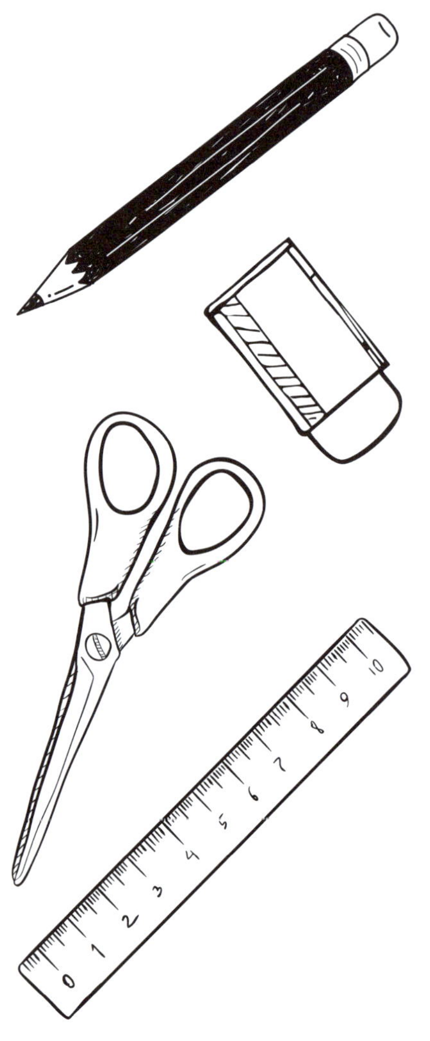

Trace over your new words.

ください	どうぞ	ありがとう
Please give me	Here you are	Thank you

きいて ください。	Please **listen**.
みて ください。	Please **look**.
たって ください。	Please **stand**.
すわって ください。	Please **sit**.
しずか に して ください。	Please be **quiet**.

What is the teacher telling you to do? Trace over the grey key words, then draw the teacher giving the command and you performing it.

THE TEACHER	YOU
たって ください。	
すわって ください。	
しずか に して ください。	

きいて ください。	Please **listen**.
みて ください。	Please **look**.
たって ください。	Please **stand**.
すわって ください。	Please **sit**.
しずか に して ください。	Please be **quiet**.

Fill in the missing words in the teacher's speech bubbles. Put a full stop (。) in the last box!

しろ	white	あお	blue	みどり	green
くろ	black	きいろ	yellow	ちゃいろ	brown
あか	red	オレンジ	orange	むらさき	purple

Trace over the colour words, then shade the animals in the given colour.

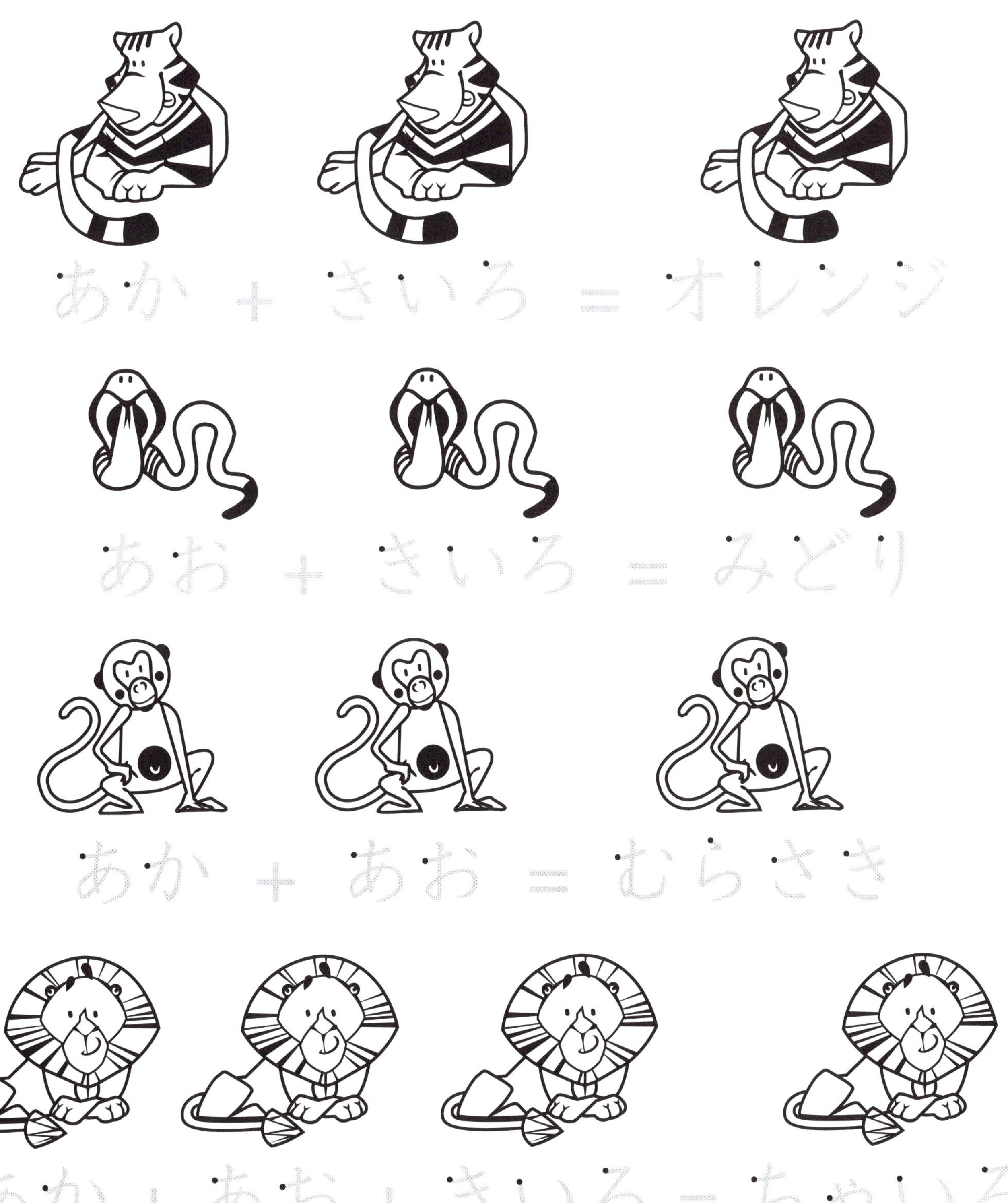

しろ	white
くろ	black
あか	red

あお	blue
きいろ	yellow
オレンジ	orange

みどり	green
ちゃいろ	brown
むらさき	purple

Colour in the picture using the correct colours.

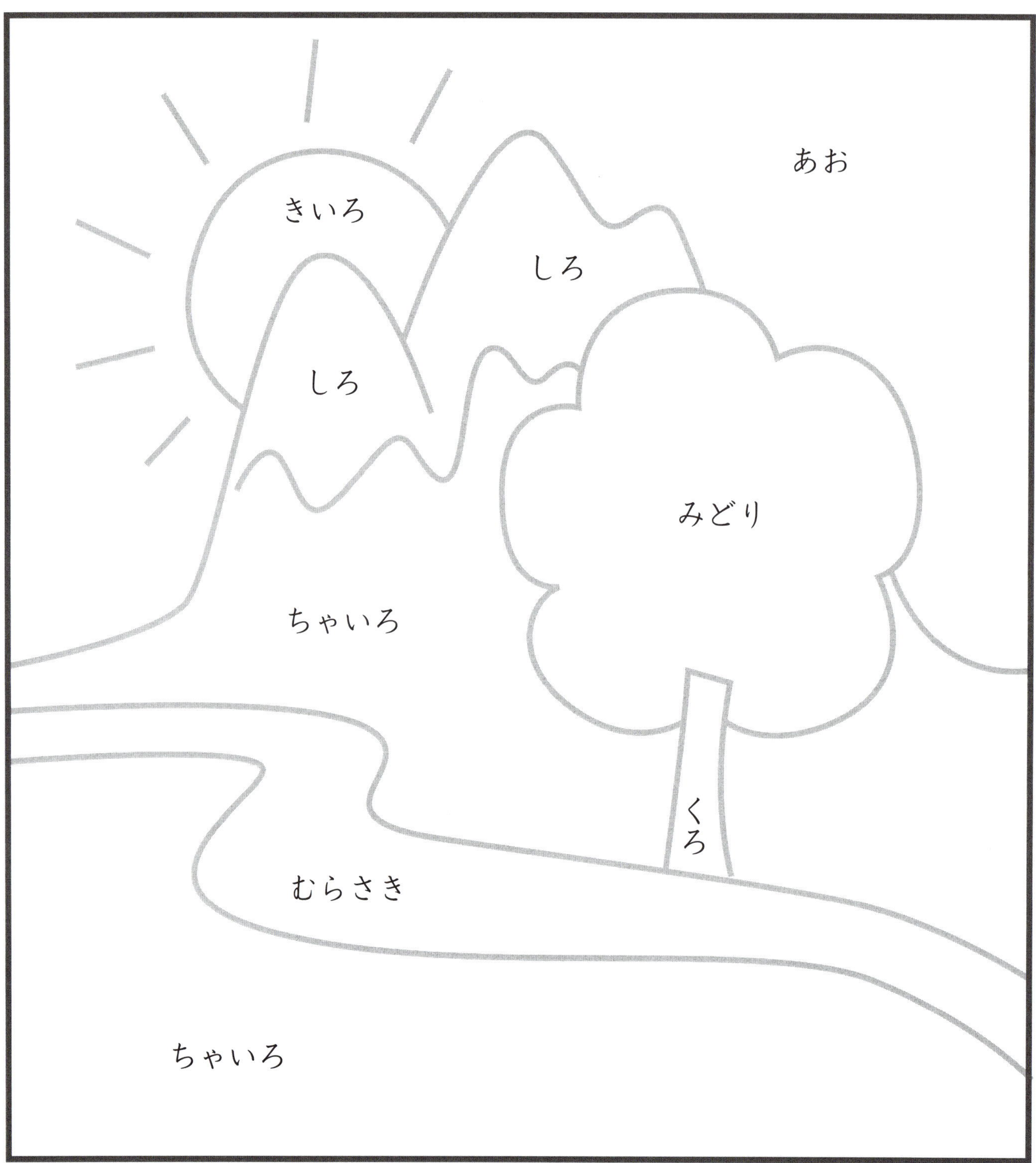

☺☺☺ がすきです。
I like ☺☺☺.

Trace over the Japanese words in the sentence, then shade over the colour words in the correct colour. What do the sentences say?

オレンジ	がすきです。

I like ____________________.

むらさき	がすきです。

I ____________________ purple.

ちゃいろ	がすきです。

I like ______________________________.

あお	がすきです。

I like ______________________________.

しろ	white	あお	blue	みどり	green
くろ	black	きいろ	yellow	ちゃいろ	brown
あか	red	オレンジ	orange	むらさき	purple

☺☺☺ が すき です。	I like ☺☺☺.

Trace over the Japanese words, then colour が すき です in あか .
What do the sentences say?

くろ が すき です。

English: ______________________________

オレンジ が すき です。

English: ______________________________

きいろ が すき です。

English: ______________________________

あか が すき です。

English: ______________________________

さる	monkey
ぞう	elephant
とら	tiger
くま	bear

きりん	giraffe
ゴリラ	gorilla
ライオン	lion
へび	snake

Find and trace over the zoo animal words in the Japanese wordsearch. Use a different colour for each animal word, then shade the matching pictures in the same colour. Look for words **across** and **down**.

ぞ	う	へ	び	く	き
う	ね	ゴ	リ	ラ	り
と	と	ら	ち	す	ん
ラ	イ	オ	ン	こ	え
く	ま	さ	る	い	ん

さる	monkey
ぞう	elephant
とら	tiger
くま	bear

きりん	giraffe
ゴリラ	gorilla
ライオン	lion
へび	snake

☺☺☺ が すき です。	I like ☺☺☺.

Look at the picture, trace over the hiragana letters, then complete the Japanese sentence. What does your sentence say in English?

☐☐ が すき です。

English: ______________________

☐☐☐ が すき です。

English: ______________________

☐☐☐ が すき です。

English: ______________________

☐☐☐☐ が すき です。

English: ______________________

ライオン	lion
ぞう	elephant
とら	tiger
ゴリラ	gorilla

あお	blue
あか	red

これは☺☺☺です。	This is a ☺☺☺.

Trace over the Japanese sentences.

Shade 

in あお, then shade 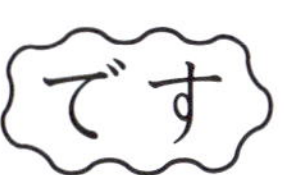

in あか.

What does your sentence say in English? The first one has been done for you.

これはさるです。

English: This is a monkey.

これはぞうです。

English: ______________________________

これはとらです。

English: ______________________________

これはゴリラです。

English: ______________________________

さる	monkey
ぞう	elephant
とら	tiger
くま	bear

きりん	giraffe
ゴリラ	gorilla
ライオン	lion
へび	snake

☺☺☺ が すき です。	I like ☺☺☺.
これ は ☺☺☺ です。	This is a ☺☺☺.

Shade the sentences with が すき です and I like in your favourite colour.

Shade the sentences with これ は and This is in a different colour.

Now join the matching sentences.

これ は ぞう です。	This is a snake.
ライオン が すき です。	This is an elephant.
くま が すき です。	This is a tiger.
これ は とら です。	I like lions.
これ は さる です。	This is a monkey.
これ は へび です。	I like gorillas.
ゴリラ が すき です。	This is a giraffe.
これ は きりん です。	I like bears.

アイスクリーム	ice-cream
チョコレート	chocolate
おかし	sweets/snacks

ケーキ	cake
ヨーグルト	yoghurt
ドーナツ	doughnut

Draw a picture in each box, then trace over the label.

アイスクリーム

ヨーグルト

おかし

ケーキ

ドーナツ

チョコレート

アイスクリーム	ice-cream
チョコレート	chocolate
おかし	sweets/snacks

ケーキ	cake
ヨーグルト	yoghurt
ドーナツ	doughnut

☺☺☺ が すき です。	I like ☺☺☺.

If you like the food in the picture, trace over が すき です and I like to make your own matching English and Japanese sentences.

アイスクリーム が すき です。
I like ice-cream.

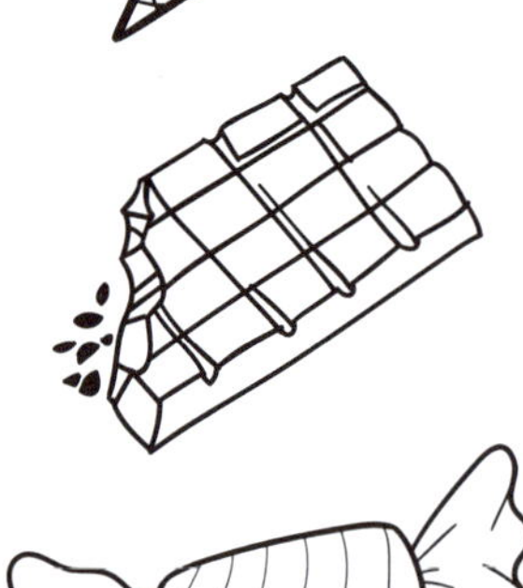

チョコレート が すき です。
I like chocolate.

おかし が すき です。
I like sweets.

ドーナツ が すき です。
I like doughnuts.

ヨーグルト が すき です。
I like yoghurt.

ケーキ が すき です。
I like cake.

おいしい	delicious
まずい	not tasty

Draw some yummy things in the おいしい box and some bad-tasting things in the まずい box, then trace over the labels.

おいしい

まずい

アイスクリーム	ice-cream	ケーキ	cake
チョコレート	chocolate	ヨーグルト	yoghurt
おかし	sweets/snacks	ドーナツ	doughnut

おいしい	delicious	です	is
まずい	not tasty	は	particle wa

Trace over the Japanese words, choosing the one in each box that makes the Japanese sentence match the English sentence.

ケーキ は
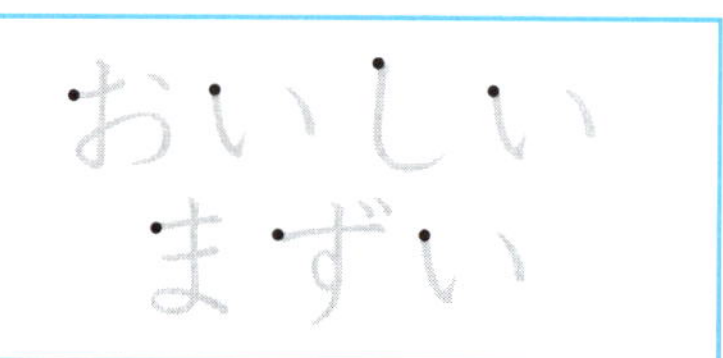

です。

Cake is delicious.

ドーナツ は
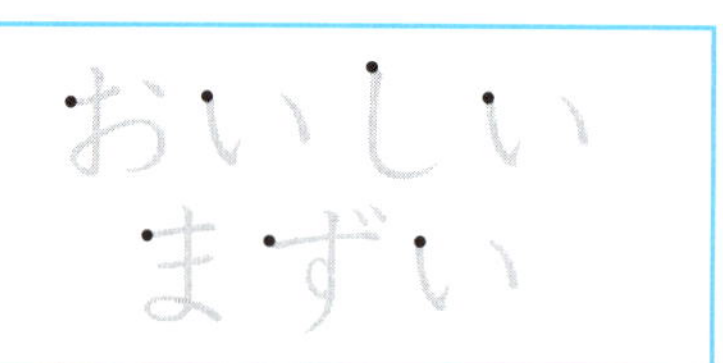

です。

Doughnuts are not tasty.

ヨーグルト は
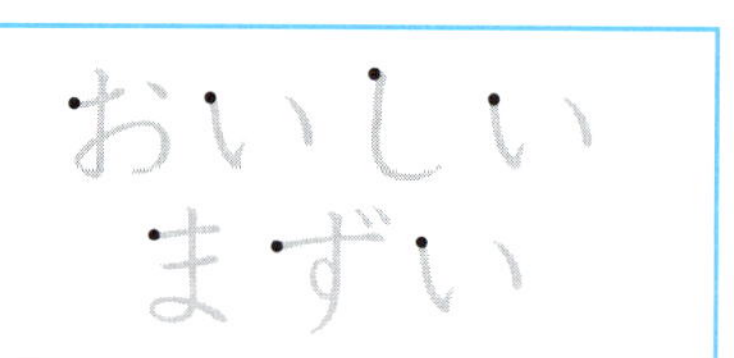

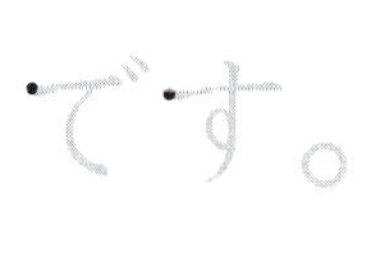

Yoghurt is delicious.

Trace over the hiragana, then write the matching romaji next to each letter.

と		す		え		う	
ぬ		ね		ち		こ	

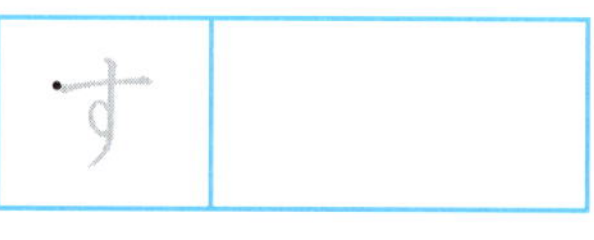

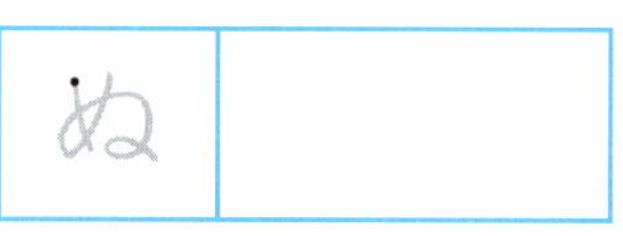

ふね	ship
ボート	boat

ヨット	yacht
カヌー	canoe

Trace over the sea transport words, then colour in the pictures.

ふね	ship
ボート	boat

ヨット	yacht
カヌー	canoe

Practise the new word ふね, then draw a picture of a ふね and trace over the label.

ふ	ね	ふ	ね	ふ	ね	ふ	ね

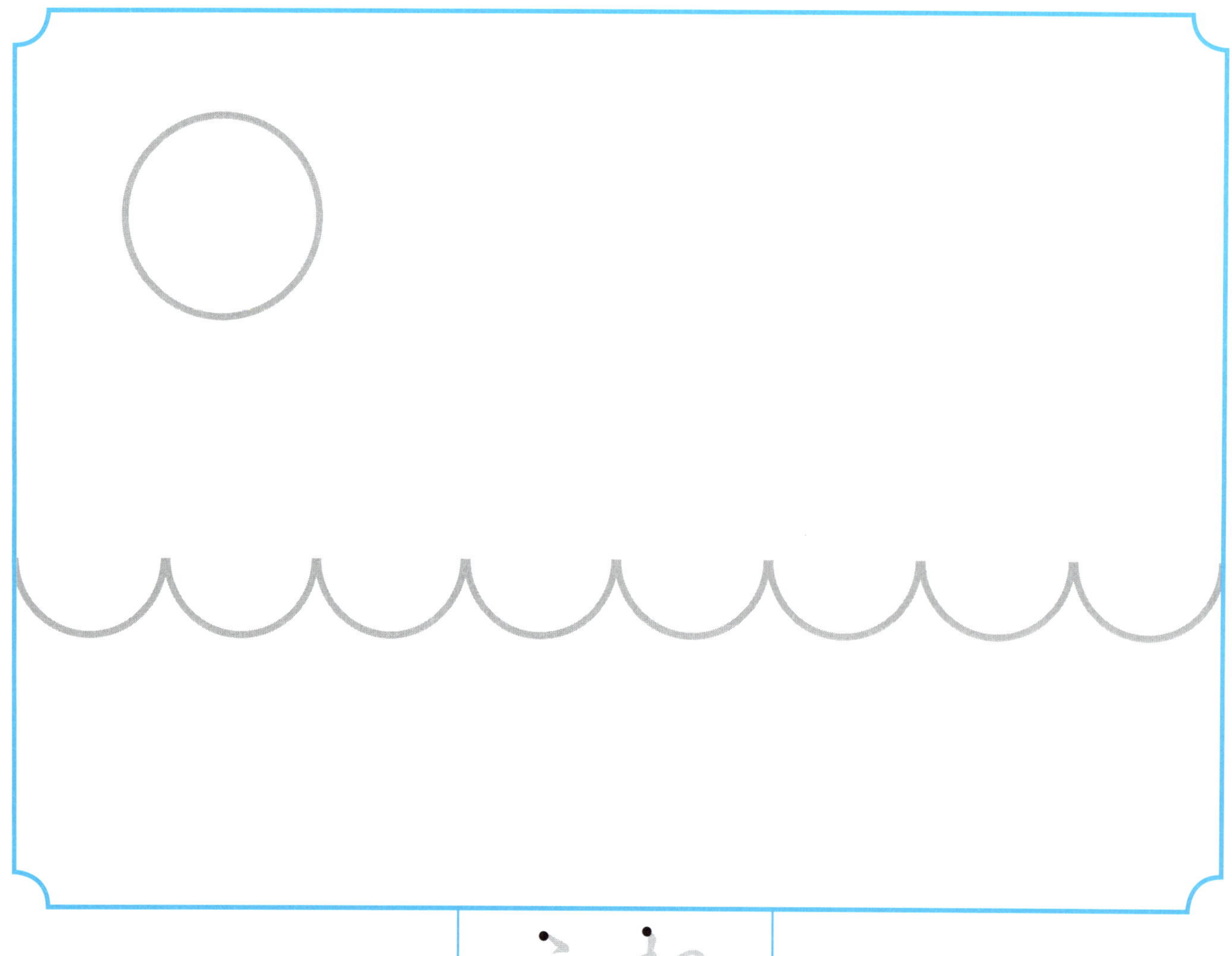

ふね

バス	bus
くるま	car
でんしゃ	train
じてんしゃ	bicycle

ふね	ship
ボート	boat
ヨット	yacht
カヌー	canoe

☺☺☺でいきます。	I go by ☺☺☺.

Trace over でいきます and I go by to make your own sentences. Fill in the missing English word, then draw a matching picture in the box.

バスでいきます。

I go by

じてんしゃでいきます。

I go by

ボートでいきます。

I go by

でんしゃでいきます。

I go by

ふねでいきます。

I go by

バス	bus
くるま	car
でんしゃ	train
じてんしゃ	bicycle

ふね	ship
ボート	boat
ヨット	yacht
カヌー	canoe

☺☺☺で いきます。	I go by ☺☺☺.

Trace over the Japanese letters, then fill in the boxes to complete the sentences.

バスで いきます。

I go by ☐ .

でんしゃ ☐ いきます。

I go by train.

ヨットで いきま  。

I go by yacht.

カヌーで いきます。

I go  canoe.

じてんしゃで  きます。

I go by bicycle.

11	十	+	一	=	十	一
12	十	+	二	=	十	二
13	十	+	三	=	十	三
14	十	+	四	=	十	四
15	十	+	五	=	十	五

Trace over the Japanese numbers, then write them yourself in the blank boxes below.

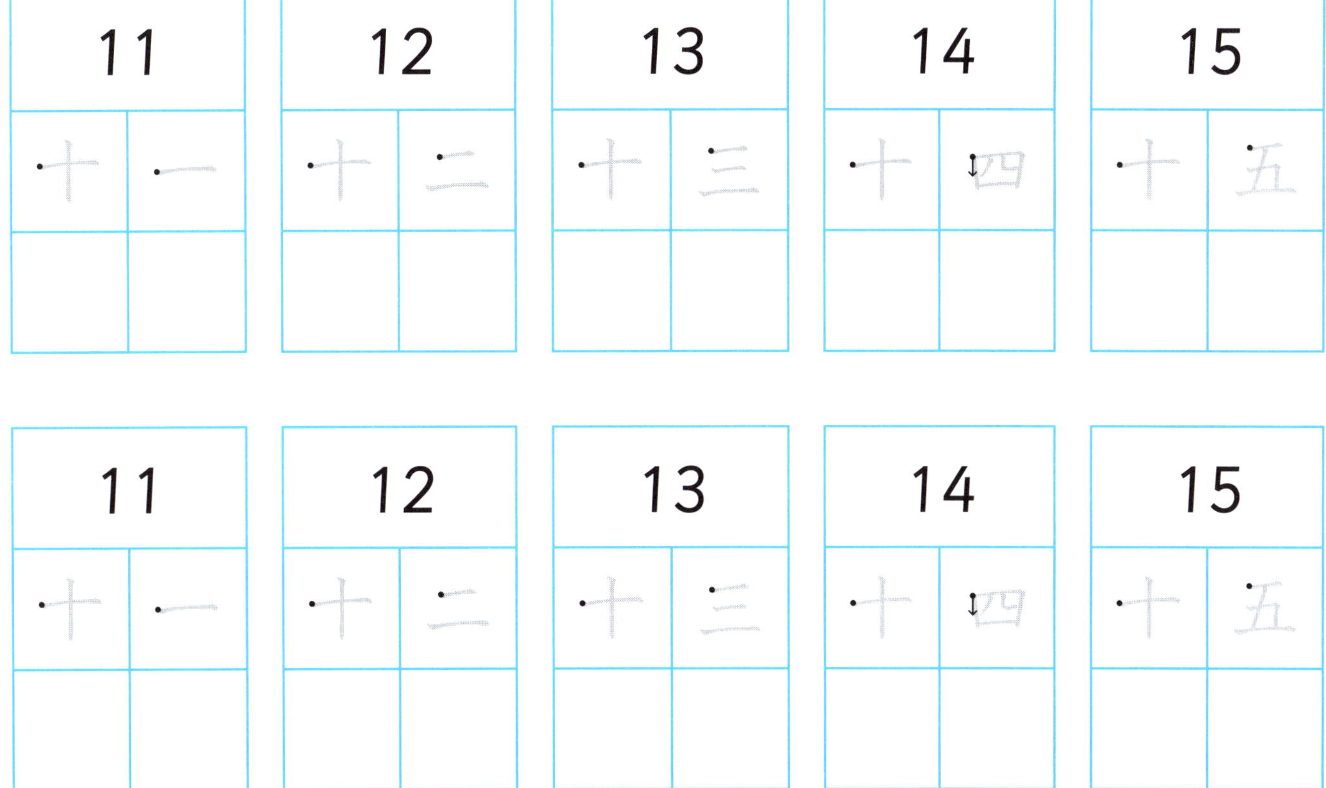

16	十	+	六	=	十	六
17	十	+	七	=	十	七
18	十	+	八	=	十	八
19	十	+	九	=	十	九
20	二	x	十	=	二	十

Trace over the Japanese numbers, then write them yourself in the blank boxes below.

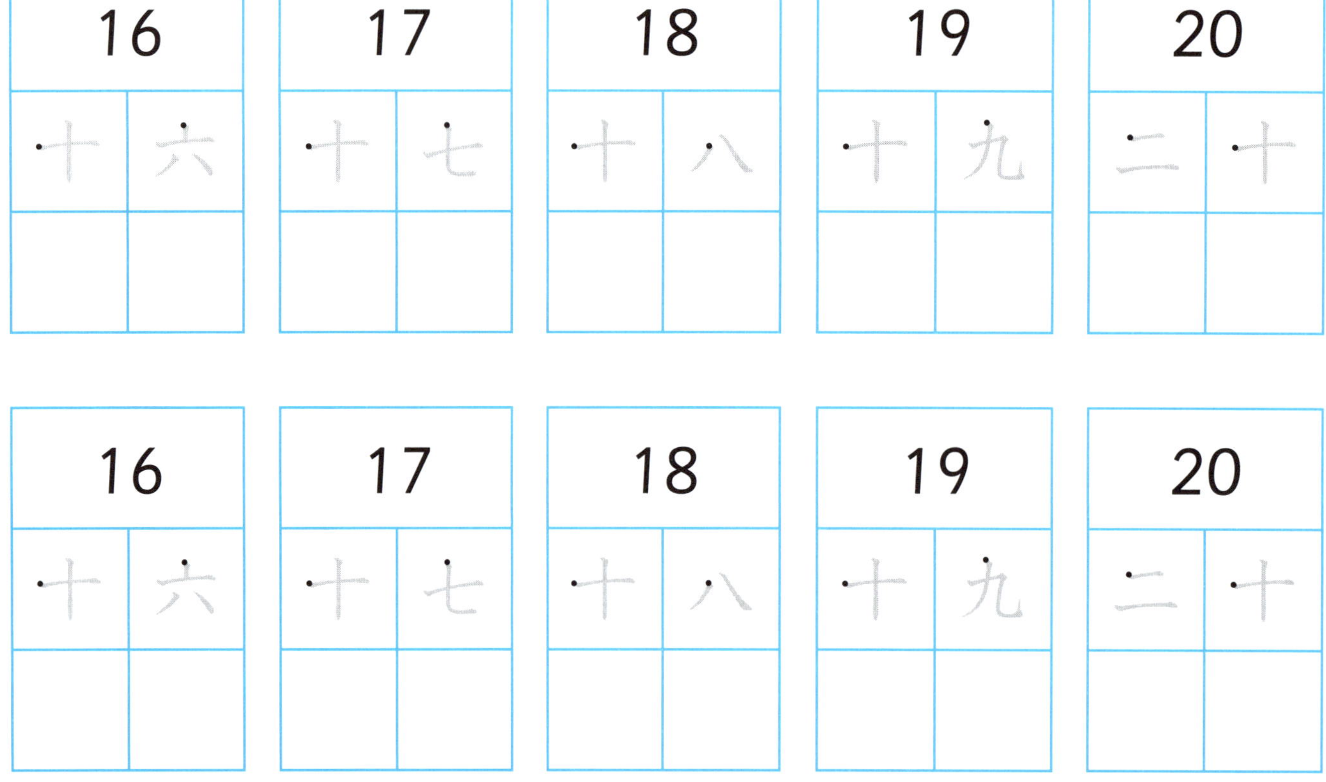

I	い	い	い	い	い	い
✍						
U	う	う	う	う	う	う
✍						

Find the hidden hiragana letters in the picture.

How many hiragana letter い did you find?	
How many hiragana letter う did you find?	

E	え	え	え	え	え	え
✍						
KO	こ	こ	こ	こ	こ	こ
✍						

Help the sumo wrestler get to the ring.

How many hiragana letter え did you find along the correct path?

SU	一	す	す	す	す	す
✍						
CHI	一	ち	ち	ち	ち	ち
✍						

Trace over the hiragana letters, then circle the correct romaji below.

ち
SU CHI

ち
SU CHI

す
SU CHI

ち
SU CHI

す
SU CHI

す
SU CHI

TO	`	と	と	と	と	と
✍						
NU	ヽ	ぬ	ぬ	ぬ	ぬ	ぬ
✍						
NE	丨	ね	ね	ね	ね	ね
✍						

Trace over the hiragana letters.

What letter have you made?

Hiragana:

Romaji:

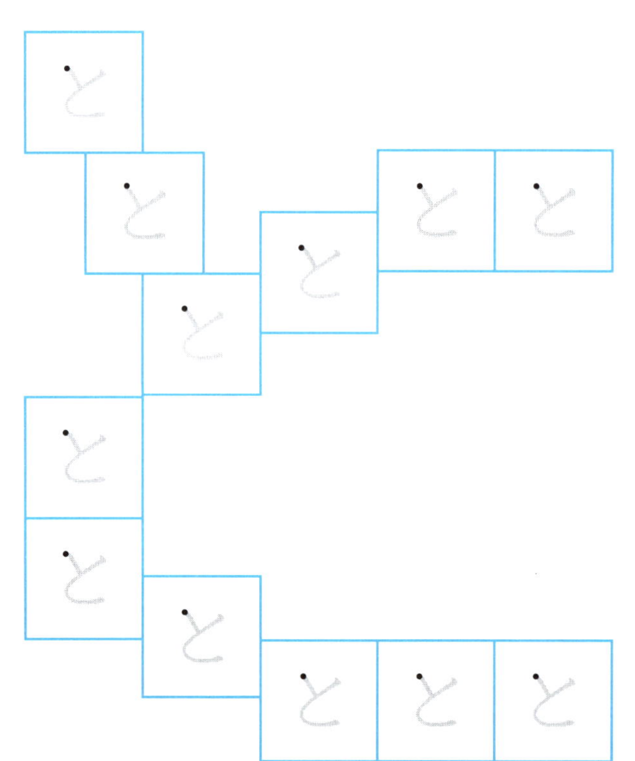

Colour the matching hiragana and romaji letters in the same colour.

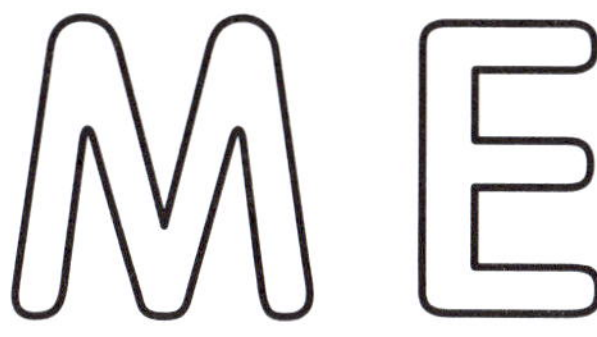

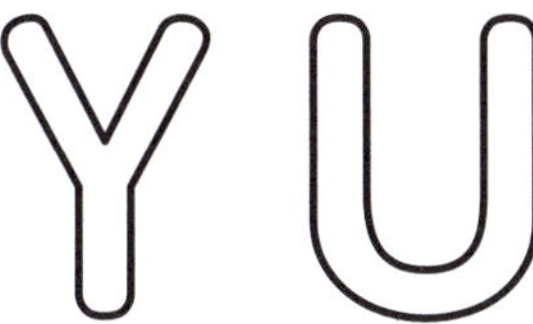

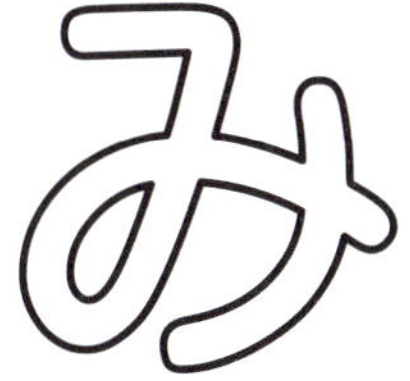

YO	ˋ	よ	よ	よ	よ	よ
✍						
RA	ˋ	ら	ら	ら	ら	ら
✍						
RI	ι	り	り	り	り	り
✍						

Turn the hiragana letters below into pictures of anything you like.

RE						れ
✍						
WA						わ
✍						

Shade the squares with れ. Draw dots in the squares with わ.

Which hiragana letter can you see?

romaji

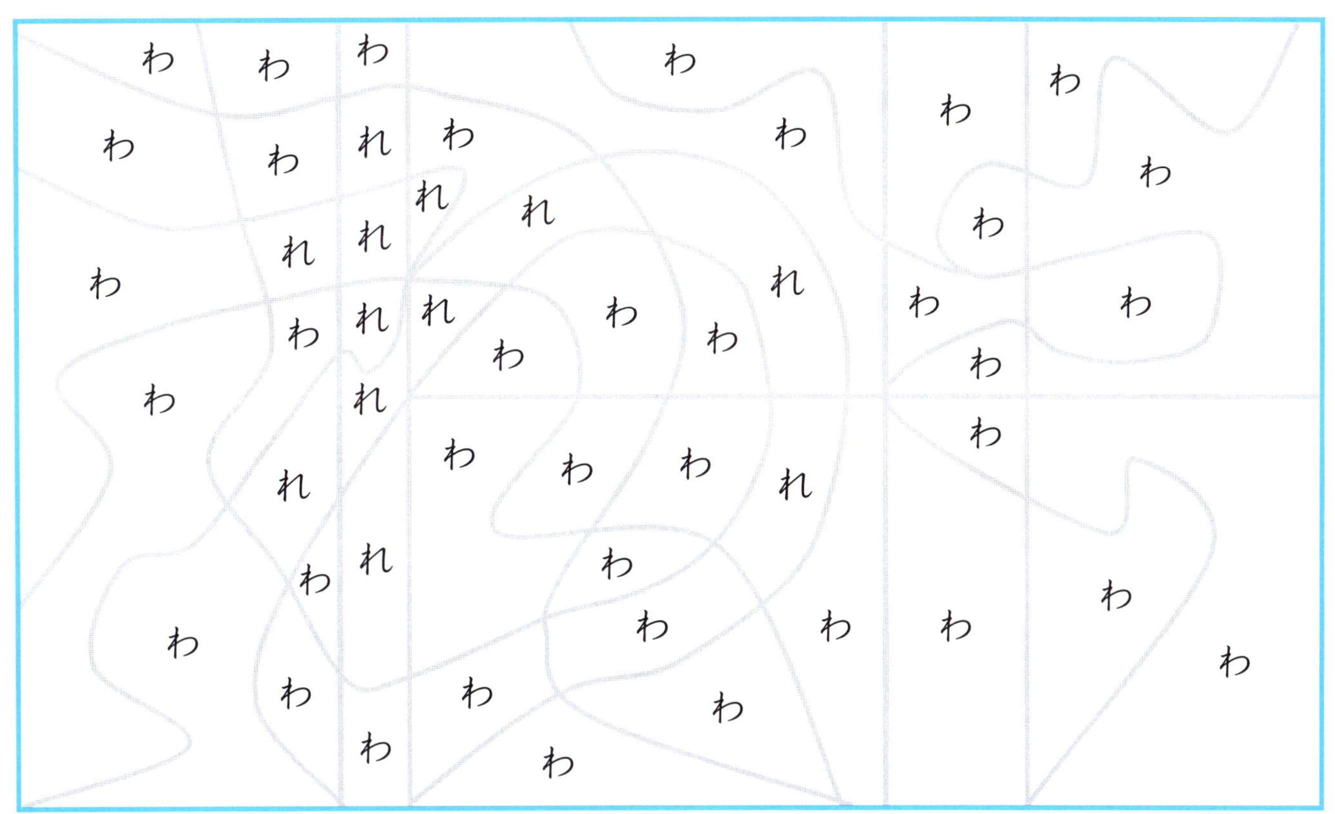

い	I
う	U
え	E

こ	KO
す	SU
ち	CHI

と	TO
ぬ	NU
ね	NE

み	MI
め	ME
ゆ	YU
よ	YO

ら	RA
り	RI
れ	RE
わ	WA

あか	red

みどり	green

Trace over the correct hiragana letters in あか and the wrong hiragana letters in みどり .

SU	す	め	れ	わ	よ
NU	よ	ら	わ	ぬ	す
ME	み	め	ゆ	す	と
YO	ぬ	ね	よ	い	え
RE	れ	と	す	ち	ぬ
WA	い	ち	こ	え	わ
I	わ	ぬ	と	い	こ
KO	め	こ	す	い	う
E	え	ね	わ	い	よ
TO	す	よ	と	え	い
MI	め	わ	と	み	よ
RA	ぬ	ね	と	め	ら
CHI	り	ち	み	わ	ら

Trace over **one** word in each box, then follow your teacher's instructions.

REVISION BINGO

おやすみなさい こんばんは	おねえさん おとうさん おかあさん	いもうと わたし ぼく
おおさか とうきょう にほん	せんせい ほん えんぴつ	あか きいろ しろ
こんにちは おはようございます	おとうと さようなら 七さいです。	おにいさん さい です

Trace over **one** letter or word in each box, then follow your teacher's instructions.

REVISION BINGO

いう	六 八 四	へ 二 ん
十六 十二 十四	七 九 十	一 三 五
十一 十五 十七	十三 十八 二十	て の ひ

Trace over **one** word in each box, then follow your teacher's instructions.

REVISION BINGO		
こんにちは おはよう ございます	おとうさん いもうと あかちゃん	かようび どようび にちようび
さようなら こんばんは しずか	おおさか とうきょう にほん	はさみ こども せんせい
つくえ えんぴつ ものさし	たって ください みてください きいて	ください どうぞ ありがとう

Trace over **one** letter or word in each box, then follow your teacher's instructions.

REVISION BINGO		
いう	くつし	てのひ
十六 十二 十四	七 九 十	へ 六 ん
えこ	十三 十八 二十	す ち 五

Trace over **one** word in each box, then follow your teacher's instructions.

REVISION BINGO

ください どうぞ ありがとう	みどり あか きいろ	すき ちゃいろ くろ
きりん ライオン へび	おとうさん せんせい あかちゃん	さる くま とら
かようび ぞう にちようび	しろ あお むらさき	これは です しずか

Trace over **one** letter or word in each box, then follow your teacher's instructions.

REVISION BINGO

と ぬ ね	て の ひ	く し そ
十八 十一 十	い う え	ゆ つ る
す ち	十三 十六 二十	三 み 四

Trace over **one** word in each box, then follow your teacher's instructions.

REVISION BINGO		
わたし ぼく です	おかし おいしい まずい	ふね でいきます
すき ちゃいろ くろ	みどり あか きいろ	くるま でんしゃ じてんしゃ
かようび どようび にちようび	にほん おおさか とうきょう	さる くま とら

Trace over **one** letter or word in each box, then follow your teacher's instructions.

REVISION BINGO

と め よ	く ゆ そ	み ち る
十八 十一 十	い う え	て ぬ れ
す ね	十三 十五 二十	わ ら り

HOW MUCH CAN YOU REMEMBER? LL 1 – 4; WL 1 – 3

LISTENING

Listen to the teacher, then circle the correct answer.

1	2	3	4	5
3 years old	hello	good evening	mother	11
5 years old	good morning	older sister	father	16
7 years old	goodnight	goodnight	baby	18

READING

Look at the cards the teacher will show you. Circle the correct answer.

6	7	8	9	10
20	3	14	I	O
12	15	8	KA	TA
9	18	19	SO	U

Look at the map of Japan. Connect the names of the two main cities to the correct parts of the map. Circle the name of the capital city.

CONGRATULATIONS! You remembered ______ things about Japan and its language.

LISTENING

Listen to the teacher, then circle the correct answer.

1	2	3	4	5
eraser ruler teacher	Sunday Please listen. Please sit.	Tuesday Friday Saturday	Please give me … Thank you. Here you are.	book scissors teacher

6	7	8	9	10
Saturday Monday Thursday	paper child ruler	Wednesday chair mother	Please give me … Please stand. desk	Please look. Please be quiet. Please sit.

READING

Look at the cards the teacher will show you. Circle the correct answer.

1	2	3	4	5
10 8 14	I U E	KO E I	E U KO	SU E CHI

CONGRATULATIONS! You remembered ______ things about Japan and its language.

LISTENING

Listen to the teacher, then circle the correct answer.

1	2	3	4	5
red blue brown	blue orange green	white yellow black	elephant giraffe bear	monkey I like blue

6	7	8	9	10
monkey lion bear	giraffe gorilla snake	This is a snake. I like green. I like snakes.	I like tigers. This is a tiger. I like elephants.	I like white. I like lions. This is a lion.

READING

Look at the cards the teacher will show you. Circle the correct answer.

1	2	3	4	5
10 8 14	I SU E	NU E TO	YU U KO	U ME KO

CONGRATULATIONS! You remembered ______ things about Japan and its language.

LISTENING

Listen to the teacher, then circle the correct answer.

1	2	3	4	5
sweets chocolate doughnuts	cake ice-cream yoghurt	delicious not tasty cake	boat canoe ship	car boat bicycle

6	7	8	9	10
bus train sweets	This is a bus. I like trains. This is a train.	I go by train. I go by boat. This is a boat.	Cakes are not tasty. Chocolate is delicious. I like cakes.	This is a cake. Yoghurt is not tasty. I like ships.

READING

Look at the cards the teacher will show you. Circle the correct answer.

1	2	3	4	5
YO RA MI	RA RI WA	YO YU WA	ME MI RE	YO RE YU

CONGRATULATIONS! You remembered ______ things about Japan and its language.

WORD LIST – ENGLISH/JAPANESE

English	Kanji	Hiragana	Romaji
1	一	いち	I CHI
2	二	に	NI
3	三	さん	SA N
4	四	し OR よん	SHI/YO N
5	五	ご	GO
6	六	ろく	RO KU
7	七	しち OR なな	SHI CHI/NA NA
8	八	はち	HA CHI
9	九	く OR きゅう	KU/KYU U
10	十	じゅう	JU U
11	十一	じゅういち	JU U I CHI
12	十二	じゅうに	JU U NI
13	十三	じゅうさん	JU U SA N
14	十四	じゅう し OR よん	JU U SHI/YO N
15	十五	じゅうご	JU U GO
16	十六	じゅうろく	JU U RO KU
17	十七	じゅう しち OR なな	JU U SHI CHI/NA NA
18	十八	じゅうはち	JU U HA CHI
19	十九	じゅう く OR きゅう	JU U KU/KYU U
20	二十	にじゅう	NI JU U

English	Hiragana/Katakana	Romaji
am	です	DE SU
baby	あかちゃん	A KA CHA N
bear	くま	KU MA
bicycle	じてんしゃ	JI TE N SHA
black	くろ	KU RO
blue	あお	A O
boat	ボート	BO O TO
book	ほん	HO N
brother (older)	おにいさん	O NI I SA N
brother (younger)	おとうと	O TO U TO
brown	ちゃいろ	CHA I RO
bus	バス	BA SU
cake	ケーキ	KE E KI
canoe	カヌー	KA NU U

WORD LIST – ENGLISH/JAPANESE		
English	Hiragana/Katakana	Romaji
car	くるま	KU RU MA
chair	いす	I SU
child	こども	KO DO MO
chocolate	チョコレート	CHO KO RE E TO
delicious	おいしい	O I SHI I
desk	つくえ	TSU KU E
doughnut	ドーナツ	DO O NA TSU
elephant	ぞう	ZO U
eraser	けしゴム	KE SHI GO MU
father	おとうさん	O TO U SA N
Friday	きんようび	KI N YO U BI
giraffe	きりん	KI RI N
goodbye	さようなら	SA YO U NA RA
good evening	こんばんは	KO N BA N WA
good morning	おはよう ございます	O HA YO U GO ZA I MA SU
goodnight	おやすみなさい	O YA SU MI NA SA I
gorilla	ゴリラ	GO RI RA
green	みどり	MI DO RI
hello (good day)	こんにちは	KO N NI CHI WA
Here you are.	どうぞ	DO U ZO
I (girls)	わたし	WA TA SHI
I (boys)	ぼく	BO KU
I am ... (used by boys)	ぼく は ... です	BO KU WA ... DE SU
I am ... (used by girls)	わたし は ... です	WA TA SHI WA ... DE SU
I am ... years old	... さい です	... SA I DE SU
ice-cream	アイスクリーム	A I SU KU RI I MU
I go by ...	... で いきます	... DE I KI MA SU
I like ...	... が すき です	... GA SU KI DE SU
Japan	にほん	NI HO N
like	すき	SU KI
lion	ライオン	RA I O N
Monday	げつようび	GE TSU YO U BI
monkey	さる	SA RU
mother	おかあさん	O KA A SA N
not tasty	まずい	MA ZU I
orange	オレンジ	O RE N JI

WORD LIST – ENGLISH/JAPANESE

English	Hiragana/Katakana	Romaji
Osaka	おおさか	O O SA KA
paper	かみ	KA MI
particle wa	は	WA
pencil	えんぴつ	E N PI TSU
Please be quiet.	しずかにして ください	SHI ZU KA NI SHI TE KU DA SA I
Please give me …	… を ください	… O KU DA SA I
Please listen.	きいて ください	KI I TE KU DA SA I
Please look.	みて ください	MI TE KU DA SA I
Please sit.	すわって ください	SU WA T TE KU DA SA I
Please stand.	たって ください	TA T TE KU DA SA I
purple	むらさき	MU RA SA KI
red	あか	A KA
ruler	ものさし	MO NO SA SHI
Saturday	どようび	DO YO U BI
scissors	はさみ	HA SA MI
ship	ふね	FU NE
sister (older)	おねえさん	O NE E SA N
sister (younger)	いもうと	I MO U TO
snake	へび	HE BI
Sunday	にちようび	NI CHI YO U BI
sweets/snacks	おかし	O KA SHI
teacher	せんせい	SE N SE I
Thank you.	ありがとう	A RI GA TO U
This is a …	これは … です	KO RE WA … DE SU
Thursday	もくようび	MO KU YO U BI
tiger	とら	TO RA
Tokyo	とうきょう	TO U KYO U
train	でんしゃ	DE N SHA
Tuesday	かようび	KA YO U BI
Wednesday	すいようび	SU I YO U BI
white	しろ	SHI RO
yacht	ヨット	YO T TO
… years old	… さい	… SA I
yellow	きいろ	KI I RO
yoghurt	ヨーグルト	YO O GU RU TO

あ	い	う	え	お
A	I	U	E	O
か	き	く	け	こ
KA	KI	KU	KE	KO
が	ぎ	ぐ	げ	ご
GA	GI	GU	GE	GO
さ	し	す	せ	そ
SA	SHI	SU	SE	SO
ざ	じ	ず	ぜ	ぞ
ZA	JI	ZU	ZE	ZO
た	ち	つ	て	と
TA	CHI	TSU	TE	TO
だ			で	ど
DA			DE	DO
な	に	ぬ	ね	の
NA	NI	NU	NE	NO
は	ひ	ふ	へ	ほ
HA	HI	FU	HE	HO
ば	び	ぶ	べ	ぼ
BA	BI	BU	BE	BO
ぱ	ぴ	ぷ	ぺ	ぽ
PA	PI	PU	PE	PO
ま	み	む	め	も
MA	MI	MU	ME	MO
や		ゆ		よ
YA		YU		YO
ら	り	る	れ	ろ
RA	RI	RU	RE	RO
わ				を
WA				O
ん				
N				

HIRAGANA COMBINATION CHART

きゃ	きゅ	きょ
kya	kyu	kyo
ぎゃ	ぎゅ	ぎょ
gya	gyu	gyo
しゃ	しゅ	しょ
sha	shu	sho
じゃ	じゅ	じょ
ja	ju	jo
ちゃ	ちゅ	ちょ
cha	chu	cho
にゃ	にゅ	にょ
nya	nyu	nyo
ひゃ	ひゅ	ひょ
hya	hyu	hyo
びゃ	びゅ	びょ
bya	byu	byo
ぴゃ	ぴゅ	ぴょ
pya	pyu	pyo
みゃ	みゅ	みょ
mya	myu	myo
りゃ	りゅ	りょ
rya	ryu	ryo